LIFE IN MONOCHROME
Poetry and Prose

Stephen Robert Kuta

Copyright

Published by Re-invention UK
Chelmsford
Essex

Copyright © 2019 Stephen Robert Kuta
www.stephenkuta.com

The moral rights of the author have been
asserted
Copyright © 2019 Re-invention UK

All Rights Reserved.

No part of this publication may be reproduced,
stored in a retrieval system, or transmitted,
in any form or by any means, without prior
permission in writing of Re-invention UK,
or as expressly permitted by law, by licence or
under terms agreed with the author.

Cover Design
By Saad Ali Copyright © 2019

A catalogue record for this book is available
from the British Library.

First Published 2019

2nd Edition
ISBN 978-0-9549899-4-1

For Peter Black
The love I share in this book
are the words I wrote for you.

Published Works

Anthologies
Paint the Sky with Stars (In remembrance to the Boxing Day Tsunami 2004)
Once I Write of Love (Selected Poetry and Prose)
War and Verse (Poetry and prose from World War One, as seen in the National Press)
Life in Monochrome (Poetry and Prose)

Photography
1978 - 2018 (My Life in Pictures)
Cape Town

History and Biography
Mrs Mary Plaskett (1739 - 1827)
Selina's Letter (Tales of Suicide from Victorian and Edwardian London)
Semper Fidelis (The Lwów Eaglets)
The Devil's Servant (The Dark Conjurer of Batcombe)

LIFE IN MONOCHROME
Poetry and Prose

Stephen Robert Kuta

I will burn myself
to keep you warm,
to keep the cold of winter at bay.
For you love, I will do that,
if all that is left is my ashes
please don't them throw away.

When you touched my lips with truth
I knew then
that you were perfect for me.

I will not let the light inside
fade and die.

I am a part of you
like the sun is a part of a glorious day,
and the stars and moon
a chunk of night.
I am with you
like a wave upon the sand
the gentle touch of my caressing hand.

To me, there can only be love.

Just like the ocean and sky
the way they kiss and touch in the
distance,
just like the sea and sky, our love too
is infinite.

Driftwood

Like driftwood, I travel.

I may sink or settle
the waves will wash over me,
Crash
beat down on me.

Poseidon's white horses
will carry me,
into darkened
deep seawater from land away from me.

I will float
for as long as the ocean does carry me,
in the arms of Triton
Orion above me.

Like driftwood, I travel.

Until the salt
the elements weather me,
the ocean drowns, takes
dissolves me.

Like Driftwood.

Isobel at the Shore of Bucaidh

To you who'd read my songs of devotion
    and only hear of pain and rage.
There is but a story of pure emotion
from the dust of history in a forgotten age.

Standing fine upon the rocks n' broken shell
    at the Shore of Bucaidh.
    Isobel
toes lapped by the salty sea.

I watched her awhile and remained unseen
    her silent beauty stead.
For our lands were a mess of things unclean
the English and Scots alike, we're dead.

Our Jacobite war had passed
now here she stood, my love so true.
virtue, fare and light at last
from death surpassed, grew a world anew.

I scowl at the stink of the rotting men,
    the decay of corpses there.
For across this craggy highland glen
our lands and homes, we're burnt now bare.

    In my loss, love was found
    hereupon the Moray Firth.
    Red haired, her beauty bound
    to the sodden highland Earth.

Monsters

I broke from the house
in the depths of my despair,
as I spoke
rage sparkled in my eyes.
My anger was unspeakable
I trembled
I fear,
I have not met them all.
The Narcissists, the self-absorbed
the self-centred, deceivers,
dispassionate of all hearts
that scavenge like ravens in the
darkest sky.
Content to take all that is dear to you
leave you broken,
empty against a barren world that is
content on creating monsters
rather than encourage love.

Nothing is more painful,
then your feelings inside.
Nothing is more painful,
then the human mind.
Sleep has no remorse
when you are truly broken.
It deprives your soul like poison,
we weep and embrace in our misery.
Over and over again
it never relinquishes.

Believe in yourself
be a free spirit.
Leap high, run, shout.

I am beautiful.
In every way imaginable

Rock bottom
taught me the lessons needed,
so slowly I climbed.
I kept going with every slip and tumble.
the view I found was beautiful.

No matter how daunting
the mountain looks.
We all have the ability to climb it.

Be whom you want to be,
as long as you are kind,
you are beautiful in my eyes.

When love is pure.
Your heart will know.

Sometimes you need to travel,
to the very edge of the world.
To find yourself
and
to love what you find.

Sometimes life is a torrent,
a River wild,
an ocean.
You are out of your depth
and
you have to swim like fuck.

Its easy to lose yourself
when the ocean swells unforgivingly.

We are just stars in our family's
constellation.

Become a beacon
of love and friendship.
Share your light across the world
For your light is beautiful.

Heaven is a kiss
but only one that is true.

Earth is being grounded,
to a place in your heart.

Live your life be free,
for the mystery of being
is not existing
but
finding something to live for.

Life
Can be
Heavy
As heavy as heaven.
Heaven
Upon the back of Atlas,
Condemned to hold up the heavy
Celestial heavens
For eternity.

Eros
Would
Have
Wept
Too.

Like Aion
Beside Gaia
I plan to spend
Eternity
Beside you.

The moon beckons
Lighting the skies,
Devouring the darkness
With its silver light.
A River like mercury
Lights the way,
Torchlit across the cold watery glass.
Choking,
The broken promises
That is now lost
In the fathoms below.
I stare into the light
And
lose myself,
In the dark recesses.

The Earth
Has stopped spinning,
The sky burns red
Across the horizon.
This road I stand upon is empty
Twisted metal
Scattered across the ruins.
In this emptiness
I am alone,
Alone as I was
When the world was full.

If only I knew, what I know
Before each lesson was done.
If only I learnt each lesson
When the lesson begun.

I gave him my heart
he burnt it.

With every lesson
We grow wiser,
as we grow wiser
We grow stronger.

That moment you left,
that moment
you Walked out on us.

After years of forgiving you
after years of self-doubt and self-blame.

Finally the last rocks crashed down on
me.

Crushing my chest for months,
it was the heaviest of all the rocks,
like a mountain on my shoulders.

We are the accumulation of the dreams
of generations.

At least once in my life, I have loved
the wrong person.

And
that love broke me.

A true positive life
Will see the light in everyone.

Fire and Ice

If the world did end in fire
Or, as cold as winter ice.
Let the love inside, inspire
Not the hatred, forfeit its price
Live your life,
What you require
Let your world suffice.
Allow your heart, what you desire
Be mistaken...
once...
Or twice.

Let others aspire.
As so too
You live.

A fusion of saffron and scarlet hue
elegantly charm the horizon.
clouds float by
I sigh and ponder
in hope they may lead me to you.

maybe love is like the sunrise
so many see it - yet so few feel it.

Just the thought of my beloved,
leads to these fingers to ache and numb
As they drown in an abundance of words,
that can only be soothed by hope.
For these sentimental eyes yearn
for love.

Love

I hope

I find it.

Come with me, my bonnie lad
Across the glen to Skye.
Rugged moors, cloud clad
Thundering rivers lie.
Stand with me, watch the world unfold
Amidst a wind-torn sky.
A chequer work of black and gold
Across the mountain high.

Come with me my bonnie lad
For all that is fair and good.

I'll never love thee more.

My sweetest boy, my darling man
  Thou heart I give to thee.
Open palm as best one can
  Holden, catch and see.
No marble walls, to keep you out
  No castle turrets soar.
No woes or ills to crow about
  I'll never love thee more.

If thou love, do give divine
  As I so give to thee.
For I am yours, so make you mine
  What will be, will be.
My fortress stands with salt and sand
  Built without a door.
It falls with care into your hand
  For Ill never love thee more.

The Fall

Alan Watts once said;
"It is crazy to fall in love"
We do not say, "rising into love."
"we fall."

We fall from a higher level
Rapidly and without control,
We lose our balance,
Collapse,
"I give myself."

If something is falling
It is becoming,
Smaller,
Or less,
"Take me."

To fall is to give ourselves
Inevitably to another person,
The fall, becomes the tie
The tie, becomes the creation.
"Do what you will with me."

To fall is a condition,
One takes a risk, on another
That in itself,
Is an act of faith.
"I am yours."

Life is an act of faith
We do not know what is going to
happen,
We do not know
If the ground beneath us will collapse.

So to love,
To fall in love is crazy,
And yet...
If people did not take that fall,
That act of faith,
Life would simply not be.

The Caulbearer

Birth and death do not dwell,
So close, so near together
Soul to the Earth with silken tether.
Allow me a life, far and old
To learn anew, wisdom unfold.

Loss of a child

Standing there barefoot
Under a mourning sky.
Standing there and waiting
Contemplating
Thinking
Grieving.
Standing there barefoot
Over a water verge.
Standing there sojourn
Yearn
Learn
Discern.
For this water, cold
Deep unforgiving
Swept my boy away from me.

Culloden Moor

The birds don't sing
On Culloden Moor
Winter, spring
Grief endure.

Low the wind, dark the mud
Across this phantom silt.
Tartan torn, flesh and blood
Fragment bone, splintered hilt.

Pale the earth, faded grey
Land of no hope, no light.
Land of dust across the way
Of those who fell with might.

Beneath the moss, bones below
Trampled men their souls endure.
Groan, weep and sorrow, woe
This land of grief called Culloden Moor.

Sadness at Christmas

So its December
Christmas not far away,
I hope you get what your heart desires
I hope its a lovely day.

I hope you will all be smiling
Laughing and having fun,
Wearing your silly hats
Pulling crackers with ya Mum.

I will be in my bedroom
Hiding so Dad can't find,
He covers me in bruises
Hits my back and behind.

Christmas is no fun
Not for my family anyway,
No toys or merry dancing
Just a normal sodding day.

So when you open your presents
Around the Christmas tree,
Give a little thought
For boys and girls like me.

A River Free

God looked down upon our plane
And found a man near death,
He sent his Angel to comfort him
To wait for life's last breath.

The Angel stayed beside you
As I held your dying hand,
Than morning came and took you
To rest in heaven's land.

His garden must be beautiful
He only takes the best,
He took you far away from us
To heaven's eternal rest.

Even though I can't see you
Father, I feel you near,
Your loving final words
Your son remembers clear.

Heaven is a lucky place
Wherever that may be,
Up above, or fishing
Along a river free.

I plan to have you in my life,
forever.
More than forever,
in the next life,
I will remember
I will look for you.
I will keep doing that
until the end of time.

Monochrome

Silent words
Resonate
Against a backdrop of grey.
Grey against a backdrop
Of words that remain silent.

White space

You are a work of art made of vibrant colour,
Not at all, black and white.
You think life is colourless and bland
And the spaces in between are white.
But in truth
You are a canvas, I promise,
Full of colour in a world of monochrome

Dark as Night

The night rides in on a horse of pure
midnight velvet,
beckoned by the stars.
As the colours of the day rest,
the hillside becomes its monochrome
beauty,
Grey shapes that make an ever-
changing,
ever-present puzzle,
The night becomes one, rock to plant to
animal,
one promise of life
awaiting the return of the sun.

Do I know you
In my soul
With my intuition,
In my gut
Or am I a fool.
To believe
That you wouldn't
Break my heart.

This
Monochrome
Film
Covers my eyes,
And I see something
Plain
And dark
And worth fearing.

Peter

Peter, snowflakes kiss our cheeks
across a white linen land
But warmth resides within.
No matter how cold and forlorn our
winters maybe.

Winter may howl and blow a chill
against our windows pane,
but blankets keep us warm
as the crackle of an open fire roars
beside us.

But no matter how cold,
or whenever winter and grey brings
pain or hardship, or challenge.

Nothing is greater
then the warmth
our hearts do bring.

My eyes
do lead
through
the dark of night
my life
through
fog and rain
winding paths
weathered
cracked
into day again.

Footprints past no longer fit
time ticks, as seasons rise
and seasons quit
years to dust carried away
by zephyr
life to rust and dust
and weather.

Five

I have loved five times
four were wrong
three went bad
two were sad
and one was over before it even begun.

The fifth
is still being written
and I plan to hold
share, care and behold
like I have never loved before.

Love like the roots that hold the trees
to the ground.
and hold the clouds in the sky.

Fuck this Monochrome World
But love every colour.

With Love

Stephen Robert Kuta x

About the Author

Stephen Robert Kuta was born in Chelmsford, Essex, England in 1978, the second eldest of five children, he is off second-generation Polish/English descent. His grandfather spent his young adult life in a Nazi Labour Camp before arriving in England in the early 1950s.

He studied English Language, Literature, History and Drama and went onto to publish prose and poetry in selected anthologies throughout the 1990s and was credited with a publication in the national newspaper, the Sunday Mirror in remembrance of Diana Princess of Wales. He eventually edited an anthology of work in 2005, a book intended to bring the voices of the world together collectively in response to the 2004 Boxing Day Tsunami. The book was of a limited run and all profits from its sale were donated to the Tsunami Earthquake Fund. The book has gone onto become a valued piece of social history and often used in university academic studies. The book now sells for high values.

Stephen continues to push boundaries in humanities and creative writing, spending much of his time managing various historical and personal blogs Online all of which have been met with praise and popularity.

Humanities have always been at the forefront of his interests, and he has continued learning with the open university focusing on the great war historically and through study with wartime literature and poetry.

www.ingramcontent.com/pod-product-compliance
Lightning Source LLC
Chambersburg PA
CBHW031501040426
42444CB00007B/1164